CHRISTIAN CHURCH AFFIRM

LGBTQ+?

The Christian church is being divided like never before over the acceptance of LGBTQ members and leaders. The question begs to be answered: is homosexuality still a sin against the Seventh Commandment of "thou shalt not commit adultery," or has the meaning of sin and its consequences been reimagined to fit the secular culture in which we live?

Understanding the definition of sin and its consequences means understanding the difference between eternal life and death! We may all have our own opinions of what constitutes sin, but the Bible clearly defines sin for us. 1 John 3:4 says,

> "Whosoever committeth sin transgresseth also the law: for sin is the transgression of the law."

This Scripture states that sin is the transgression or breaking of the Ten Commandment law of God.

My goal in writing this little book is to help people understand the God-given responsibility of the last-day Christian church and how it applies to sin and sinners. I can start by saying that it is NOT the church's responsibility to judge the human heart. 1 Samuel 16:7 says,

> "For the Lord seeth not as man seeth. For man looketh on the outward appearance, but the Lord looketh on the heart."

The church of God should be a hospital for sinners and a sanctuary for the hurting to be nurtured and loved through all of life's ups and downs. The church is all about mending broken people through the good news of salvation and deliverance from a sin-sick world.

WHAT DOES GOD EXPECT OF CHRISTIANS?

In Matthew 28:18-20, Jesus commissioned His disciples to go to the ends of the earth proclaiming the gospel, teaching, baptizing, and making disciples in the name of the Father, Son, and Holy Spirit. I call it the "Go Ye Commission!" It is as relevant today as ever before in Earth's history. As Christians, we are to prepare a lost and dying world for the return of our soon-coming Savior. When Jesus returns to Earth, He is coming back for a people who have given their hearts and souls to Him and are keeping His commandments.

"And, behold, I come quickly; and my reward is with me, to give every man according as his work shall be. I am Alpha and Omega, the beginning and the end, the first and the last. Blessed are they that do his commandments, that they may have right to the tree of life, and may enter in through the gates into the city" (REVELATION 22:12-14).

The Bible describes these saints of God like this:

"These are they which came out of great tribulation, and have washed their robes, and made them white in the blood of the Lamb" (REVELATION 7:14).

I believe you and I are living in the closing moments of Earth's history. God is looking for people willing to stand up against any and all attacks on His church by the devil and his earthly agents.

I can tell you for sure that there is a great controversy between Christ and Satan, and today, the enemy is invading the Christian church with false doctrine like never before. Thus, I have named this book "Can The Christian Church Affirm LGBTQ+?" We will see what the Bible says. In this study, we will only use the Bible as our guide. I will not attempt to reinterpret Scripture to fit my viewpoint. We are seeking truth. Jeremiah 29:13 says,

> "And ye shall seek me, and find me, when ye shall search for me with all your heart."

I want to make a point that is sometimes overlooked by those in the church and those without. While 1 Samuel 16:7 tells us that man cannot judge other men's hearts, God does call His church to judge bad fruit that can spoil his faithful followers. We'll examine this more fully in a bit (Matthew 7:16-18). Isaiah 62:6,7 says,

> "I have set watchmen on your walls, O Jerusalem; They shall never hold their peace day or night. You who make mention of the Lord, do not keep silent, and give Him no rest till He establishes and till He makes Jerusalem a praise in the earth."

Watchmen were sentries stationed on a wall or in a tower to look out for and warn of dangers approaching far and near. It is imperative that we Christians continue as watchmen on the wall to protect the church from being deceived by the devil's agents, sometimes dressed in the cloak of Christianity. A good Christian watchman, such as a pastor or leader of any church, is called to watch what goes on spiritually, physically, and culturally in the church. They should pray for wisdom and sound the alarm when perceived spiritual or cultural transgressions occur within the church of God. Ezekiel 33:6 says,

"But if the watchman sees the sword coming and does not blow the trumpet, so that the people are not warned, and the sword comes and takes any one of them, that person is taken away in his iniquity, but his blood I will require at the watchman's hand."

Again, these Scriptures emphasize the responsibility of spiritual leaders to be alert and sound the alarm when danger approaches.

A CATEGORY CHANGE

In recent years, the LGBTQ movement has grown by unprecedented leaps and bounds. Until the last 20-30 years, the vast majority of people (including many government leaders and medical professionals) perceived homosexuals and transgender people to be cultural outcasts with mental illness! Nearly every government worldwide has had laws in place for hundreds of years forbidding open homosexual relationships between people of the same sex and same-sex marriages. It's not that many years ago that if a transgender man was dressing and acting as a woman in public, he was arrested and sent to jail!

In fact, until 2013, the Diagnostic and Statistical Manual (DSM) in all its study material, openly stated that Gender Identity Disorder was a mental illness! That has all changed in the last decade or so. Can you imagine the DSM and American Psychiatric Association (APA) have changed their decades-old evaluations of Gender Identity Disorder as a mental illness based on current politics and culture rather than cognitive, medical, or scientific findings? They admit the reason they decided to change the name to Gender Dysphoria was to remove the stigma attached to transgender people as being mentally ill.

Wow! Why not change the name "alcoholic" (the term used to describe individuals who have developed a chronic physical and psychological dependency on alcohol) to "social drinker?" Does changing the term "alcoholic" change the fact that he is an alcoholic?

Does changing the name of a man who apparently thinks he is a woman to the point that he will dress up as a woman, go out in public, and try to pass as a woman reverse his mental illness? Of course not! How far can this kind of thinking continue in society until almost everyone is confused? If I have a problem stealing, wouldn't it be better if the police changed the term to describe me from "thief" to "an incessant borrower?" Maybe they wouldn't arrest me for stealing! Hopefully, you get my point. The government and the APA seem to have acquiesced to the transgender community by re-categorizing a mental illness into the "normal" behavior category.

The LGBTQ movement is a group of people that represents a small minority of the population. Despite this, they have organized into a powerful lobby that wields great influence over government officials to change their laws. Even medical professionals turn a blind eye to the scientific fact that there is no "Queer DNA Gene" which biologically determines that people are born queer. The LGBTQ movement linked themselves with the civil rights movement to gain more support. But the LGBTQ group, though a minority, is not comparable to Black people, White people, or any other race. Race is unchangeable and not subject to choice. Since science tells us there is no "Queer DNA Gene," those identifying as queer can change their mental state and sexual preference through the power of the Holy Spirit. I know this for sure, as I have met numerous formerly "gay" men and women. They are a testament to the fact that when they surrendered their life to Jesus Christ, He gave them victory over identifying as LGBTQ. For some, it didn't happen overnight, but it did happen. They now live normal heterosexual lives. Thanks be to the Lord Jesus Christ!

THE CHURCH'S PROBLEM WITH LGBTQ

I can tell you that I love people, including LGBTQ people. I have friends and family who openly lead homosexual lives, and I love them dearly! The government has passed laws to protect them from the discrimination they faced in the past. That's a good thing as long as these laws don't infringe on the rights of the majority as well. Former President Barrack Obama championed same-sex marriage all the way to the Supreme Court here in America, making it the law of the land. Therefore, the LGBTQ community has the right to live their lives the way they choose as long as they live within the laws of the land.

Many LGBTQ people identify themselves as Christian. And they have a legal right to reinterpret Scriptures however they choose. Religious freedom is a great thing. The potential problem between the Christian Church and the LGBTQ population is that they practice a way of living that is in direct opposition to God's Ten Commandment law, which is a pillar of the Christian faith. The problem is amplified when the LGBTQ community demands that the Christian church affirm them and their lifestyle.

While most Christian churches do open their doors to the LGBTQ for attendance and fellowship, they do not accept them as members or leaders of their churches because of the incompatibility of their religious beliefs. Yet, what we are seeing is the LGBTQ community has become very aggressive in their push for acceptance in the church. Now, the church is faced with a big problem. Do we compromise in the name of inclusion, fairness, equity, and diversity? Or are we morally bound to accept the pillars of the Christian faith, which are built on the Bible and the Bible only?

Christians are admonished to love everyone, and not to discriminate against any person. Each soul is equally important in God's sight. He loves the saint and the sinner. Keep in mind, He hates sin but loves the sinner (which we will discuss in more detail in a moment). So, the valid question is: can the Christian church affirm LGBTQ? It is an increasing concern because of the growing numbers of LBGTQ who now identify themselves as "Christian." The church has some tough decisions to make in this matter, but the Bible provides us with the clear answer. It is vital that we take the right scriptural approach, as these people are not our enemies, and their eternal security hangs in the balance.

It seems that more and more Christians are buying into the idea that the LGBTQ should be accepted as members in God's church. We have to stand firmly on Bible Scriptures concerning this subject. We as a church must look beyond our emotions. When we look at the big Bible picture, it's the same message as it has always been. We must love people enough to tell them the truth and be watchmen on the wall to protect the church from ungodly advances of the enemy to deceive the flock. 1 Corinthians 6:9-11 (NKJV) says,

> "Do you not know that the unrighteous will not inherit the kingdom of God? Do not be deceived. Neither fornicators, nor idolaters, nor adulterers, nor homosexuals, nor sodomites, nor thieves, nor covetous, nor drunkards, nor revilers, nor extortioners will inherit the kingdom of God. And such were some of you. But you were washed, but you were sanctified, but you were justified in the name of the Lord Jesus and by the Spirit of our God."

WHO IS OUR REAL ENEMY?

The truth is, as Christians, we cannot compromise God's laws to be politically or culturally correct. We should remember that our fight is not against other people. We are in a spiritual battle with the devil! He alone is our enemy. Ephesians 6:12 says,

> "For we wrestle not against flesh and blood, but against principalities, against powers, against the rulers of the darkness of this world, against spiritual wickedness in high places."

And, according to 1 Peter 5:8, we must

> "Be sober, be vigilant; because your adversary the devil, as a

roaring lion, walketh about, seeking whom he may devour."

And in John 10:10, Jesus spells it out very clearly:

"The thief (the devil) cometh not, but for to steal, and to kill, and to destroy: I am come that they might have life, and that they might have it more abundantly."

These Scriptures tell us that the devil, who is "the thief," will use any means possible to deceive, divide, and destroy God's Church. Satan has found an opening to accomplish his sinister goals through the LGBTQ movement. In truth, there is no new biblical "light" discovered in the Bible in recent years that proclaims that the homosexual lifestyle is no longer a sin.

Yet, in the last decade, acceptance of LGBTQ by the Christian church is nothing short of alarming for those considered Bible-believing Christians. If the biblical view of homosexuality has not changed to disqualify it from still being listed as an abominable sin to God, who or what has changed? Why are many Christians now embracing (and some even celebrating) that which was considered a sin of perversion only a few years ago, breaking the Seventh Commandment?

A warning flag that something is amiss should be going up in the minds of Christian believers everywhere! We all know the world's constant political and cultural changes are now infiltrating the church. I'm sure I am not the only one who has noticed that the Christian church has trouble labeling the LGBTQ lifestyle as a sin. We as a church still label things like adultery, pedophilia, drugs, alcoholism, rape and murder, stealing, and lying all as sins, and we have no problem placing those things in the "sin basket." But, for some reason, it seems we cannot, or will not, put the LGBTQ lifestyle in the "sin basket."

Folks, once again, the church cannot and must not bow to political correctness. I don't care how popular or politically correct it is: allegiance to race, culture, and politics is a road that will lead to eternal death! The Christian church, cannot forgive sin! Only God can forgive sins! Like God, the church should love sinners but hate the sin. When we, as a church, affirm same-sex /LGBTQ relationships or any other open sin, we become followers of Satan instead of Christ. Why? Because we are attempting to stand in the place of God forgiving sins!

Plus, think about this: even God does not forgive unconfessed sins! One of the identifying marks of the antichrist spirit is a group that claims to forgive sins. Let's read Mark 2:5-7,

> "When Jesus saw their faith, he said unto the sick of the palsy, 'Son, thy sins be forgiven thee.' But there was certain of the scribes sitting there, and reasoning in their hearts, 'Why doth this man thus speak blasphemies? Who can forgive sins but God only?'"

Blasphemy against God, according to Mark 2:5-7, is when humans, church, or laity claim to forgive sins. Revelation 13:5, referring to the beast power, reads,

> "And there was given unto him a mouth speaking great things and blasphemies..."

According to Merriam-Webster Dictionary, blasphemy is defined as "the act of insulting or showing contempt or lack of reverence for God; and or the act of claiming the attributes of a deity."

One of God's attributes, of course, is that He forgives sins! The day any Christian church approves, endorses, or affirms the homosexual practice or any other open sin, we too, will be guilty of claiming to forgive sins. Folks, please hear me. I'll repeat it: God's church does not have the authority to forgive sins.

Sinful human beings cannot bless open sin! Remember, it was

One of my favorite Bible Scriptures is 2 Chronicles 7:14, which says,

> "If my people, which are called by my name, shall humble themselves, and pray, and seek my face, and turn from their wicked ways; then will I hear from heaven, and will forgive their sin, and will heal their land."

This Scripture clarifies that Jesus only forgives our sins when we TURN FROM our wicked ways. He will not forgive unconfessed, unrepented sins.

GOD'S ORIGINAL PLAN

Let's take a look at the Christian church's biblical position on the topic of LGBTQ. We should start at the beginning of the book of Genesis to get the Bible's perspective of this fast-growing part of society closing in on the church doors. Some churches have already accepted the LGBTQ as Christian members and leaders into their churches. There are still many Christian churches that I'm aware of that are standing as watchmen on the wall, sounding the alarm, giving a wake-up call that deception and error are nigh at hand, even at the door! And there are many church members and leaders who are extremely quiet on this subject, as they don't want to offend anyone or be "canceled." One of the problems dividing the church on this issue seems to be that many members, and maybe especially the younger children, seem to be confused about whether the Bible is clear that the practice of homosexuality fits into the sin category. The Bible is crystal clear on this subject! Ignorance, emotions, and social media seem to be the most prominent factors clouding the minds of many Christians when it comes to a "thus saith the Lord!" I hope and pray you will completely understand this clear biblical truth when you finish reading this book! Let's start from the beginning of the Bible. It tells us in Genesis 1:27-28,

"So God created man in his own image, in the image of God created he him; male and female created he them. And God blessed them, and God said unto them, Be fruitful, and multiply, and replenish the earth, and subdue it: and have dominion over the fish of the sea, and over the fowl of the air, and over every living thing that moveth upon the earth."

Then, in Genesis 2:24, God says:

"Therefore shall a man leave his father and his mother, and shall cleave unto his wife: and they shall be one flesh."

1 Corinthians 7:2 states,

"Nevertheless, to avoid fornication, let every man have his own wife, and let every woman have her own husband."

Ephesians 5:22-33 highlights the roles and responsibilities of husbands and wives within the context of marriage. There is not one biblical example of a husband and wife as two males or two females.

The Bible has solid evidence that proves that God created Adam and Eve, male and female, and told them to be fruitful and multiply. Two genders only! Male and female. They come together as one flesh through marriage to procreate children to replenish the earth. People of the same sex coming together cannot be fruitful and multiply.

It has never been God's intention that there be homosexual men or women having sex with one another. What purpose would it serve? Certainly not to multiply the human race! No children can be the product of men having sex with men or women having sex with women!

The devil, the Father of lies, is deceiving people into believing that homosexual relationships are affirmed and ordained by God just as heterosexual marriage relationships are. As gently as I can say this:

there is nothing natural about two men having sex when neither man is built for receiving the seed that procreates life with God's blessings. Do you see what's missing? It is God's blessing! Again, not one Scripture in all the Bible supports homosexual relationships.

We are going to examine several Scriptures showing that these relationships are not built on love, but carnal! While man continues to fall prey to sin and is heading on a downward spiral path, God, in His love for fallen man, made a way of escape from eternal death to eternal life. It is called the Plan of Salvation.

The Plan of Salvation, in essence, equals restoration for the soul of man. Since man chose to sin, why would God even bother to restore him? Romans 5:8 says,

> "But God commendeth his love toward us, in that, while we were yet sinners, Christ died for us."

And Jeremiah 31:3 states,

> "I have loved you with an everlasting love; I have drawn you with loving-kindness."

1 John 4:7-8 tells us,

> "Beloved, let us love one another: for love is of God; and every one that loveth is born of God, and knoweth God. He that loveth not knoweth not God; for God is love."

Once we accept Jesus Christ as Lord and Savior of our life and accept His free gift of salvation through confession and repentance of sin, we become known as a "Christian." In short, our duty and privilege is to love God and love one another. Jesus says in Matthew 22:37-39,

> "Love the Lord your God with all your heart and with all your soul and with all your mind. This is the first and great

commandment. And the second is like unto it: "Thou shalt love thy neighbor as thyself."

THERE IS VICTORY IN JESUS

I can tell you that it is the church's responsibility to teach that salvation from the wages of sin comes from confession and repentance to Jesus for any and all sins. In this little book, we will discuss various types of sin, including obvious and intentional wrongdoing, as well as instances where we may not intend to sin but still fall short, as even Paul himself admitted to struggling with. We will also learn from Scripture that there is no sin too big or too bad that God cannot or will not forgive! God is all about forgiveness, restoration, and victory over sin. Yes, we are all born with fallen, sinful natures passed on to us by Adam. Have you perhaps struggled with certain sins that have beset you for as long as you can remember? Have you prayed about them but, as of yet, haven't found victory over those sins? I want to encourage you that God can give you victory over any and all sin.

1 Corinthians 10:13 is so encouraging! It says,

> "No temptation has overtaken you except such as is common to man; but God is faithful, who will not allow you to be tempted beyond what you are able, but with the temptation will also make the way of escape, that you may be able to bear it."

This is excellent news!

> "Let no one say when he is tempted, 'I am tempted by God'; for God cannot be tempted by evil, nor does He Himself tempt anyone" (JAMES 1:13, NKJV).

Our righteous and loving God does not tempt you. The devil is the one tempting you. But he cannot make you sin. The act of sin is a choice! It makes no difference if you fell into a particular sin passed down because of your ancestors' examples or for any other reason. God says He will make a way of escape from this sin that besets/controls you! That's a big praise the Lord!

James 1:14-15 goes on to say,

> "But every man is tempted, when he is drawn away of his own lust, and enticed. Then when lust hath conceived, it bringeth forth sin: and sin, when it is finished, bringeth forth death."

The good news is that God has promised to make a way of escape. He will give you victory over any sin that is robbing you of peace and joy in your life. Sin does not satisfy the soul. Only Jesus can satisfy your soul! You and God are a winning team! We will not succumb to temptation if we are in union with God.

Since Adam and Eve's fall in the garden, humanity has been full of trouble. Sickness, tragedy, violence, and death are the result of sin. But Jesus made it clear that trouble is part of living in this world of sin. John 16:33 tells us,

> "These things I have spoken unto you, that in me ye might have peace. In the world ye shall have tribulation: but be of good cheer; I have overcome the world."

Christians should understand that temptations, trouble, and strife are all part of this life. I'm always encouraged when I read Psalm 119:165,

> "Great peace have they which love thy law: and nothing shall offend them."

Wow! Is it possible that NOTHING will offend those who love

the law of God? Actually, it is. I learned many years ago that no one can offend you! No, they can't. How often have you talked to people who say, "I haven't been to church in years because the preacher offended me!" Or, a person tells a judge, "He offended me when he called me a name, so I punched him in the nose!"

What I get from Psalm 119:165 is that being offended is a choice. Yes, that's right! You and I, through the grace of our Lord, can choose not to be offended. The behavior of others should not affect our health or interrupt our peace of mind, etc. How can we find this great peace? This Bible Scripture spells it out plainly and beautifully:

"Great peace have they which love thy law.."

The Psalmist said it this way:

"The law of the Lord is perfect, converting the soul: the testimony of the Lord is sure, making wise the simple. The statutes of the Lord are right, rejoicing the heart: the commandment of the Lord is pure, enlightening the eyes" (PSALM 19:7-8).

When we are one with Christ, the devil cannot rob us of our peace and joy.

I told you earlier that we would be using a lot of Scripture. Well, here's another beautiful Scripture to hang on to:

"I am the vine, ye are the branches: He that abideth in me, and I in him, the same bringeth forth much fruit: for without me ye can do nothing" (JOHN 15:5).

We cannot overcome sin without trusting God to bring us through! And the opposite is that as long as we are "the branches" of Christ, we can overcome even lifelong sins! I realize as humans, we are just scratching the surface of the love of God and the victory He can bring us when we put our trust in Him! But someday, we'll understand it better by and by! We already discovered the Bible defines sin in 1 John 3:4 as the breaking or transgression of God's Ten Commandment law. So now let's consider what is common to all humanity.

WHO IS GUILTY OF SINNING?

The answer to that question is given in Romans 3:23:

"All have sinned and come short of the glory of God."

Therefore, no one is perfect. Thus, no one is exempt. The devil does not want people to know the truth about sin and its consequences. The Bible's definition of sin has taken a backseat to many in the church as they've made social justice, culture, equity, and inclusion their new religion. And some are afraid to call sin by its proper name for fear of the woke/cancel culture group. "Cancel culture" is a phrase contemporary to the late 2010s and early 2020s that refers to a culture in which those deemed to have acted or spoken unacceptably are ostracized, boycotted, or shunned. Sadly, "cancel culture" has also found its way into the Christian church! We must not lose focus that the devil's goal is to divide the church of God on this earth. If the church is divided by culture and politics, it will also be divided as to what constitutes sin.

Let's find out what the Bible says about sin's consequences. We can read the answer in Romans 6:23,

"For the wages of sin is death, but the gift of God is eternal life through Christ Jesus our Lord."

So, now we understand from Scripture that breaking the Ten Commandment law of God is called sin (1 John 3:4). Since God is sinless, we can understand that sin separates us from God. Next, we learned that ALL have sinned. (Romans 3:23). Now, the question that begs to be answered is, how can one be saved from the consequences of sin? The answer is found in 1 John 1:8-10,

> "If we say that we have no sin, we deceive ourselves, and the truth is not in us. If we confess our sins, he is faithful and just to forgive us our sins, and to cleanse us from all unrighteousness. If we say that we have not sinned, we make him a liar, and his word is not in us."

Praise the Lord that He has made a way for sinful man to escape death and claim the free gift of salvation! I, too, am a sinner saved by His marvelous grace!

If we think about it, sin only falls into two categories: confessed and unconfessed. Confession + repentance of our sins to Jesus = forgiveness! Praise the Lord! Unconfessed, unforgiven, open sin will ultimately meet with the deadly consequences referred to in Romans 6:23. Christians need to understand that the "calling out of sin" is one of the main reasons for the church's existence! Not judging the human heart as we already talked about, but "calling out" or bringing attention to sins that will keep humanity from eternal life. These sins result from actions brought on by an individual's choices.

When we, the church, see sins committed by ignorance or open rebellion within the church or without, it is our duty to respond in a loving way that points people to Jesus and the keeping of His commandments! I can tell you from nearly forty years of ministry that there is no easy or popular way of calling out sin! Those openly living their lives in opposition to the Ten Commandment law of God are usually the ones most offended by this kind of preaching.

It was that way when Jesus was on earth, and it is still the same today. One could say that Jesus was definitely the target of the "cancel culture" group of His time on earth. Why? Jesus boldly called out their open sin against the commandments of God. In Matthew 15:7-9,

Jesus called out the hypocrisy of the scribes and Pharisees.

"Ye hypocrites, well did Esaias prophesy of you, saying, This people draweth nigh unto me with their mouth, and honoureth me with their lips; but their heart is far from me. But in vain they do worship me, teaching for doctrines the commandments of men."

Of course, He spoke the truth, but these leaders hated Him for exposing their sins. They decided to cancel Him. Notice some critical points of this Scripture.

"In vain do they worship me…"

Folks, this refers to those who claim to be followers of Jesus. This is not talking about non-Christians. Jesus is saying here that groups of people are worshipping in the name of Jesus. Yet, He rejects their worship! Why? Because they are honoring him with their lips (talk) but their hearts are far from Him. This is obviously referring to people who "talk the talk, but don't walk the walk."

Some people, including preachers, think this is negotiable. It is NOT! As we just read, Jesus said,

"In VAIN do they worship me teaching for doctrines commandments of men" (emphasis added).

Folks, we can have the happiest, loudest, rip-roaring church service imaginable, and everyone feels great as emotions run high. It can be a church service where people are testifying, some speaking in tongues, and people are falling down on the floor at the command of the preacher's hand, yet the church can still be void of the Holy Spirit! Jesus is nowhere to be found! God's true Christian church will affirm all of God's Ten Commandment laws. John 14:15 says,

"If you love me, keep my commandments."

Jesus often rebuked the scribes and Pharisees as He knew their worship was in vain. They were introducing and elevating the commandments of men set forth by the church leaders of their day. The spirit of God was not found in their synagogues/churches espousing commandments of men. Can you see that the same thing is happening in today's culture?

Today, the LGBTQ group within the Christian church is working feverishly to try to alter the Ten Commandments to fit their preferred perspective. They are elevating their own beliefs instead of the Word of God by promoting open sin to be affirmed by the Christian church.

Again, please notice that the LGBTQ group is not introducing new Bible scriptures to support their lifestyle choices. It is not about a "thus saith the Lord." This acceptance in the Christian church results from media and culture infiltrating the church of God. Churches buying into the acceptance/affirmation of LGBTQ are literally making decisions based on feelings, emotions, politics, or culture.

In fact, several affirming churches excuse their affirmation of LGBTQ as being about recognizing and accepting individuals as they are without judgment or discrimination. Some are appointed as deacons, elders, teachers, and even pastors. Really? I've never heard of a church affirming a known thief just as he is and inviting him to be the church treasurer without judgment or discrimination. And I've never heard of a church affirming a working prostitute just as she is and asking her to lead out in the children's department without judgment or discrimination. Or maybe affirming an alcoholic to be the church's head elder without judgment and discrimination.

I hope you get the point. I could give you many more examples, but I don't think it's necessary right now. My question would be: why doesn't the church affirm everyone just as they are without judgment or discrimination? The members and leaders of the affirming church would probably jump to be watchmen on the wall in the case of the thief, prostitute, and alcoholic.

SATAN'S STRATEGIES

God established marriage at Creation. The LGBTQ agenda for the church is to do away with God's designed marriage between one man and one woman (holy matrimony) just like they did when the Supreme Court of the United States made same-sex marriage the law of the land. It's almost unbelievable to me that men of the cloth can justify throwing the Seventh Commandment out the window in the name of fairness, equality and inclusivity. Folks, wake up! This is no time for the Christian church to fall asleep at the wheel!

The devil works within the church when he sees division among church members. He has found great support from many churches willing to drop their biblical standards to be socially and culturally acceptable. For the Christian church, this is no time to fall asleep! The prophetic book of Revelation prophesies the devil's attacks on God's last-day people. Revelation 12:17 says,

"And the dragon was wroth with the woman, and went to make war with the remnant of her seed, which keep the commandments of God, and have the testimony of Jesus Christ."

The dragon referred to here represents Satan, and the woman represents the "true church" of God. The remnant of her seed represents God's last day church on earth before the second coming of Christ. YES, we are living in the closing moments of Earth's history. To be the remnant church of God on this earth, we must remain faithful to keeping all of God's commandments as a witness to the world.

CHRISTIANS HAVE A DUTY TO CALL OUT SIN

Being a Christian carries a significant amount of responsibility. We are to

"Cry aloud, spare not, lift up thy voice like a trumpet, and shew my people their transgression, and the house of Jacob their sins" (ISAIAH 58:1).

It is essential for the saints of God to see that the calling out of open sin is a command of God. How can we as a church remain silent as we watch people so deceived by the devil that they are introducing all kinds of demonic sins into the church, leading people to a Christ-less grave? Look at what God says in Ezekiel 3:18:

"When I say unto the wicked, Thou shalt surely die; and thou givest him not warning, nor speakest to warn the wicked from his wicked way, to save his life; the same wicked man shall die in his iniquity; but his blood will I require at thine hand."

As Christians, we must not be silent!

Jesus was full of love and compassion while on Earth, yet loved people enough to tell them to go and sin no more (see John 8:11). Yes, even Jesus made many enemies because He called out the sins of people who were the religious leaders of His time on earth. The devil had his cancel culture group crying, "Crucify Him, crucify Him!" It is also true that people will hate you and me as we stand up for Christ against the grain of politics, religiosity, and culture. 2 Timothy 3:12 says,

"Yea, and all that will live godly in Christ Jesus shall suffer persecution."

SOME CHURCHES SEND MIXED MESSAGES

As we already mentioned, the religious culture during Jesus's time on Earth was more about serving the laws of man than the laws of God. It is much the same today. Therefore, Jesus, the Cornerstone of life and love, was rejected by men and sent to die on the cross. The good news is that when we study the plan of salvation, we find that Jesus willingly gave His life for man. No one took it! Oh, what a Savior!

Think about this: given the choice by the government leaders to save the life of the sinless Jesus or the life of the notorious criminal, Barabbas, the unruly mob chose to save the life of Barabbas (Luke 23:18-24). This rejection of Jesus by the mob and some of the factions in the church remains today. And yet, even though men rejected Him, God's love found a way for His creation to be saved. In fact, He has made it easier to be saved than to be lost! John 3:16 says,

> "For God so loved the world that He gave His only begotten son that whosoever believeth in Him should not perish, but have everlasting life."

What an incredible promise that only a God of love could make to such a rebellious, stiff-necked, sinful people, unworthy of anything but death! Yet, He loved us enough to make a plan of salvation to seek and save the lost. As a longtime Christian, I'm disappointed that many church leaders and some denominations send a mixed message to the unchurched when it comes to keeping the Ten Commandment law of God.

Some argue that the Ten Commandments were nailed to the cross, so now they keep them in their hearts as part of the New Covenant instead of obeying them as part of the Old Covenant. Well, my answer is: of course, we keep the Ten Commandment law of God in our hearts today, and praise God, no more lambs' blood must be shed as an atonement for our sins. It was the ordinances and ceremonial laws which were nailed to the cross (Colossians 2:14).

But the fact is, any way you slice it, the Ten Commandment law of God is still in effect today, 2000 years after the cross. Am I right? You can have all the theological discussions you want to, but it is still a sin to steal, kill, commit adultery, lie, covet, etc. It's the same today as it was before Jesus died on the cross. The Christian church must stand firm on the validity of the Ten Commandment law of God in the 21st century, or as my Dad used to say, "We should just shut up and sit down!" Remember, where there is no law, there is no sin.

Time in this book does not allow a study of the Old and New Covenants, but I do think it's essential that, as Christians, we should be the defenders of the Ten Commandment law of God. It's crucial for us to understand that the Ten Commandments were NOT nailed to the cross when witnessing to unbelievers.

Think about this: if the Ten Commandments were nailed to the cross, there would be no sin. Right? We've already shown that sin is the transgression or breaking of the Ten Commandment law of God (1 John 3:4). So, if there is no law, there is no sin. And if there is no sin, there is no need for a Savior. And if there is no need for a Savior, then there is no need for churches or preachers.

I hope you see where I am going. As Christians, we must understand that God's Ten Commandment law is eternal. Otherwise, we cannot point out sin based on our personal opinions and values. The Ten Commandments are based on Jesus Christ, the foundation's cornerstone, the Rock of Ages.

IS HEAVEN INCLUSIVE?

When we allow the Bible to guide us, we find it's not all that difficult to determine what sin is and how it affects everyone. I realize the topic of this book may not be a popular message to some, but, if we, the Christian church, are indeed God's representatives on earth, we cannot affirm or accept members, teachers, preachers, or any other persons or group of people who are in open rebellion to the Ten Commandment law of God.

The Christian church, by design, is not an all-inclusive group. No, it isn't. As Christians, we are to live by spiritual laws, which often conflict with the physical laws set up by man. Here's the problem. Present politics and culture headed by the woke/cancel culture group are aggressively lobbying to convince the Christian church to affirm everyone, even if their lifestyle is in open rebellion to God's Word. When the church refuses to compromise on issues of morality from groups such as the LGBTQ community, they accuse us of being bigots, hypocrites, homophobes, racists, or some other objectionable names.

So, let me clear this up. Jesus preached about a very non-inclusive heaven. A heaven that does not include or affirm anyone who refuses to admit they are sinners and accept His free gift of salvation through confession and repentance. The LGBTQ community denies their lifestyle is a sin. Therefore, there is no reason to repent.

This is total deception! Guided by the Holy Spirit, the apostle Paul explains the dilemma,

"Wherefore God also gave them up to uncleanness through the lusts of their own hearts, to dishonor their own bodies between themselves: Who changed the truth of God into a lie, and worshipped and served the creature more than the Creator, who is blessed for ever. Amen. For this cause God gave them up unto vile affections: for even their women did change the natural use into that which is against nature: And likewise also the men, leaving the natural use of the woman, burned in their lust one toward another; men with men working that which is unseemly, and receiving in themselves that recompence of their error which was meet. And even as they did not like to retain God in their knowledge, God gave them over to a reprobate mind, to do those things which are not convenient; Being filled with all unrighteousness, fornication, wickedness, covetousness, maliciousness; full of envy, murder, debate, deceit, malignity; whisperers, backbiters, haters of God, despiteful, proud, boasters, inventors of evil things, disobedient to parents, without understanding, covenantbreakers, without natural affection, implacable, unmerciful: who knowing the judgment of God, that they which commit such things are worthy of death, not only do the same, but have pleasure in them that do them" (ROMANS 1:24-32).

It's astounding that the LGBTQ community can read these verses and claim that woman-to-woman and male-to-male sex is blessed/ordained by God. That's an incredible deception!

We can plainly see from these Scriptures that God does not affirm people "in" their sins. God only affirms us when we ask him to forgive us "from" our sins! The push for LGBTQ acceptance and affirmation in the Christian church is much more progressive than most realize. Much of this "push" for LGBTQ acceptance comes from our higher learning institutions, such as Christian academies, colleges, and universities. Many of our professors have compromised the Word of God in exchange for acceptance from the secular world. And many of our Christian universities are more concerned about government funding and accreditation than they are with "holding down the fort," as it were, from the attacks of the enemy. Some of our Christian universities are now having what is called "Lavender" graduations. This is a special graduation for LGBTQ students attending these universities!

Now, I have no problem with the LGBTQ community attending Christian churches and being students in our schools. The problem is many Christian schools are affirming these students' lifestyle choices in the name of inclusion. Nothing is being taught in these institutions about grouping the LGBTQ lifestyle in the sin category with other sins such as drug and alcohol use and pre-marital sex. Political correctness and government pressure do not even allow these Christian universities to call for repentance from the sin of the LGBTQ lifestyle.

Many Christian universities even allow Gay and Lesbian clubs on campus. Yet, these same administrations would never allow sexually-oriented heterosexual clubs on campus or alcoholic clubs encouraging other students to participate or indulge in sex and alcohol! Many young people surveyed in Christian educational systems now support same-sex marriage and the LGBTQ lifestyle. We, as Christians, have obviously failed in our duty to properly instruct them in the ways of the Lord. Again, our silence on these life-and-death issues in the church makes us as guilty as those promoting them!

Now let's read 2 Thessalonians 2:10-12.

"And with all deceivableness of unrighteousness in them that perish; because they received not the love of the truth, that they might be saved. And for this cause God shall send them strong delusion, that they should believe a lie: That they all might be damned who believed not the truth, but had pleasure in unrighteousness."

This clearly tells us that when individuals reject the Holy Spirit long enough, God will send a strong delusion and let them believe a lie and be damned (see Matthew 12:31-32)! Now, I must insert here that these Scriptures are NOT just talking about the LGBTQ community. These Scriptures apply to any one of us who openly rebels against God's law and refuses the Holy Spirit's loving rebuke. God is a God of mercy, but He also knows when the human heart is so hardened that it will not change. Therefore, He allows the sinner to continue in his sin without the hope of repentance. This is why it is so important that we continue to search for truth. It would behoove all of us to continue to study the beautiful plan of salvation to fully understand that confession and repentance of sin to Jesus are the key ingredients to eternal life.

As we previously read, 1 Corinthians 6: 9-11 states,

"Know ye not that the unrighteous shall not inherit the kingdom of God? Be not deceived: neither fornicators, nor idolaters, nor adulterers, nor effeminate, nor abusers of themselves with mankind. Nor thieves, nor covetous, nor drunkards, nor revilers, nor extortioners, shall inherit the kingdom of God. And such were some of you: but ye are washed, but ye are sanctified, but ye are justified in the name of the Lord Jesus, and by the Spirit of our God."

This is beautiful! As Paul says in verse 11, "And such WERE some of you…" This statement shows us that through Jesus Christ, we can obtain victory over sin. Notice He didn't say, "And some of you are recovering alcoholics, thieves, fornicators, adulterers, or effeminates, etc." He said, "And such WERE some of you…!" Praise the Lord! Once again, while God hates these sins, He loves us enough to forgive us our sins when we are sorry and confess and ask forgiveness for them. Yes, we are washed in the blood of the Lamb, and His Spirit sanctifies us.

I won't apologize for being so redundant on the fact that God, in His love for fallen man, is waiting to forgive us and throw our sins into the sea of forgetfulness! I want to go back for a moment to 1 Corinthians 6:9 to talk about the word "effeminate." Are you familiar with this word? Many aren't. Let's start with the dictionary definition of effeminate: "With reference to a man having characteristics and ways of behaving traditionally associated with women and regarded as inappropriate for a man."

I'm pretty sure you've seen the transgender man who pretends to be a woman on the Bud Light TV commercial. In my opinion, he qualifies as a perfect example of effeminate. Any transgender man pretending to be a woman is definitely effeminate! Verse 9 states that abusers of themselves with humanity will not be included with those going to heaven. This and several other Scriptures refer to men bedding with men and can even include sodomy! Leviticus 18:22 says,

"Thou shalt not lie with mankind as with womankind: it is abomination."

The Bible couldn't be more explicit that God created Adam and Eve, not Adam and Steve, as they say. This is the natural order of things. Any sex, male-to-male or female-to-female, is an abomination to our Creator God! As we already read, marriage was established at Creation by God Himself. Matrimony is a holy institution between one man and one woman—period (see Genesis 2:24).

As some of you may already know, there is significant effort within the so-called "Christian" LGBTQ movement to reinterpret or reimagine Scriptures such as those we have been reading here. Many in the LGBTQ movement argue that they were "born this way," and therefore, the LGBTQ lifestyle is affirmed by God. But I have to tell you that we are ALL born with a fallen and sinful nature. However, here again, God promises to give us victory over all sin.

"For the LORD your God is the one who goes with you to fight for you against your enemies to give you victory" (DEUTERONOMY 20:4).

Friend, Jesus wants to save you from your sins no matter what they are. Please invite Jesus into your life today. Ask Him for victory in your life over the sins that are holding you back from having the relationship with Him that gives you joy, peace, happiness, and victory.

OPEN REBELLION vs. THE STRUGGLE

We've talked about open, unconfessed sins. Let's talk about the sins we don't want to do, but like Paul, we find ourselves doing. Romans 7:19-25 explains it like this:

"For the good that I would I do not: but the evil which I would not, that I do. Now if I do that I would not, it is no more I that do it, but sin that dwelleth in me. I find then a law, that, when I would do good, evil is present with me. For I delight in the law of God after the inward man: But I see another law in my members, warring against the law of my mind, and bringing me into captivity to the law of sin which is in my members. O wretched man that I am! who shall deliver me from the body of this death? I thank God through Jesus Christ our Lord. So then with the mind I myself serve the law of God; but with the flesh the law of sin."

Paul confessed that, on his own merits, he could not live up to the Ten Commandment law. But he thanked God for being the only One who can deliver him. Paul was upfront with us that he was warring between the spirit and the flesh. For a deeper understanding of the war between the flesh and the spirit, read Romans chapter 8. It confirms that we only find victory over sin through Christ.

Now let me ask: do you see the difference between open rebellion against God's law and a Christian's spiritual struggle with the flesh as we travel down life's pathway? Answer: it's the forgiveness factor! If I acknowledge and confess my sin to God, He forgives it, which is a forgiven sin. If I sin and don't confess to God and don't ask forgiveness, then it is unforgiven sin. Let me ask: can I go to heaven if I celebrate my sins, refuse to be sorry, and confess my sins to God? The answer is a resounding "NO!" No one will meet the Lord in the air on Judgement Day who has lived a lifestyle contrary to the Word of God. But for all of us like Paul, who are sinners despite ourselves and petition God to forgive us our sins,

"He is faithful and just to forgive us our sins and cleanse us from all unrighteousness" (1 JOHN 1:9).

ARE WE "JUDGING" OTHERS?

Some of you may be asking me. "Who are you to judge?"

Matthew 7:1-5 says,

> "Judge not that ye be not judged." For with what judgment ye judge, ye shall be judged: and with what measure ye mete, it shall be measured to you again. And why beholdest thou the mote that is in thy brother's eye, but considerest not the beam that is in thine own eye? Or how wilt thou say to thy brother, Let me pull out the mote out of thine eye; and, behold, a beam is in thine own eye? Thou hypocrite, first cast out the beam out of thine own eye; and then shalt thou see clearly to cast out the mote out of thy brother's eye."

Now you, the reader, may be asking: "After reading those verses, why would you then judge groups such as the LGBTQ groups? Doesn't the Bible say you are to judge not?" Yes, it does, and we already read 1 Samuel 16:7:

> "…for the Lord seeth not as man seeth; for man looketh on the outward appearance, but the Lord looketh on the heart."

So, according to Scripture, we cannot judge another man's heart. For instance, have you met a person and your first thought is, "Wow, he looks like an alcoholic!"

Now, I'm just being honest. It may be true this person may appear as someone who has abused his body with alcohol or drugs for many years. But because I don't know the individual, I have no right to judge his heart. It's possible that he was, in fact, a former alcoholic or drug abuser but is now a Christian who found victory through Jesus Christ. Let's take this scenario a little further. I may even see this man drunk and lying in a gutter, and still, I cannot judge his heart. He may love Jesus but just suffered a setback on his Christian journey. Instead of judging him, I should reach out to him in compassion and love. It may be the difference in his eternal life or possibly my eternal life!

In answer to your question, however, we have the right and responsibility as Christians to judge good fruit from bad fruit. Matthew continues a few verses later in Matthew 7:16-18.

> "Ye shall know them by their fruits. Do men gather grapes of thorns, or figs of thistles? Even so every good tree brings the forth good fruit; but a corrupt tree brings forth evil fruit. A good tree cannot bring forth evil fruit, neither can a corrupt tree bring forth good fruit."

So, let me ask: is Matthew contradicting himself, or can we reconcile both Scriptures from the same Bible writer, taken from the same chapter? Yes, we can reconcile them.

Now, if the same man that we just discussed claimed to be a Christian and celebrated the fact that he abuses his own body through the use of drugs and alcohol and demands that your church affirm him and his lifestyle by voting him into church membership and ordaining him as an elder, would your church affirm his sin and welcome him into the church membership? Of course not! Why not? Because he is openly transgressing God's health laws. Ordaining him as an elder would inappropriately indicate to the youth that abusing your body through drugs and alcohol is an acceptable lifestyle for the Christian. Please follow me now. At this point, you did NOT judge his heart. You judged his bad fruit! This is the righteous judgment John talks about in John 7:24,

> "Judge not according to the appearance, but judge righteous judgment."

Does this make any spiritual sense to you? Okay, let me word it like this: in the first example, we have no right to judge the man's heart. Only God can do that. In our second example of the same man, we can base our judgment on his bad fruit, which is open defiance of God's health laws by destroying his body through drugs and alcohol. He refuses to admit that he is living in sin but demands the church affirm him in his sin and not from his sin. This is not consistent with Christian principles. Therefore, the Pastor, the church board, and the members should be watchmen on the wall defending the church from the destructive influence this man is trying to bring.

Let's look at this from another angle. There's a knock on your front door. You look out the peephole and see a man standing there with a gun pointed in your direction. Now you are faced with a decision: do you open the door or not? Now, you could reason that maybe he wants to sell you some Girl Scout cookies as you don't really know the intent of his heart, or does your common sense kick in and you make a quick decision based on the bad fruit (gun)he is pointing your way and call **911**? As the Christian church, spiritually speaking, we should "call **911**" when we see bad fruit knocking on our church doors!

When the LGBTQ community demands that we affirm open, outright sin in the name of fairness, inclusion, race, diversity, and politics, and when their teachings deceive or mislead others away from the Word of God, we can and should counteract the counterfeit! The devil knows his time is short, so he is working quickly to separate God from His people through deception. But praise the Lord; the devil has no power over God. We belong to our Creator God.

Romans 8:38-39, says:

"For I am persuaded, that neither death, nor life, nor angels, nor principalities, nor powers, nor things present, nor things to come, Nor height, nor depth, nor any other creature, shall be able to separate us from the love of God, which is in Christ Jesus our Lord."

Isn't that incredible? No power on earth, including the devil, can separate us from the love of God!

Another popular lie is that virtually everyone will go to heaven.

So, let's set the record straight. God loves everyone, but everyone claiming to be a Christian will not enter heaven. Let's look at a couple more Bible Scriptures. Luke 13:24 says,

"Strive to enter through the narrow door; for many, I tell you, will seek to enter and will not be able."

And Matthew 7:21:

"Not everyone that saith unto me, Lord, Lord, shall enter into the kingdom of heaven; but he that doeth the will of my Father which is in heaven."

We must follow God's righteous counsel to enter into heaven. Also, let's read Jude 1:7,

"Just as Sodom and Gomorrah and the surrounding cities, which likewise indulged in sexual immorality and pursued unnatural desire, serve as an example by undergoing a punishment of eternal fire."

Many more Scriptures confirm that no one will go to heaven openly sinning against God.

THE CHURCH'S COMPROMISE

I'm amazed that the present culture demands acceptance by the Christian church of open sin, as described above. Jesus does not and will not condone open sin, nor can His church here on Earth! Heaven will be filled with those who are washed in the blood of Christ. Everyone there will have confessed and repented of their sins and accepted Jesus as Lord and Savior of their life. I find it more than interesting that the LGBTQ group is the only group that I know of that demands their sexual sins be overlooked and affirmed by the

Christian church. Drunkards, extortioners, abusers, idolaters, adulterers, thieves, liars, rapists, etc., do not have any organized group of supporters demanding God's church on Earth to affirm their sins. As Christians, we must understand that we are in a spiritual battle.

We should never be discouraged when we are butting heads against the devil. Ephesians 6:12 reminds us that we are in a spiritual warfare that cannot be won in the physical/flesh. We have to base our beliefs on the Word of God, which is spiritual. We only get sidetracked by the devil when he can tempt us to get caught up in our emotions.

As I mentioned earlier, I believe the reason the LGBTQ movement has made such inroads into the Christian church is that many of us are compromised because we have friends or relatives who are living the LGBTQ lifestyle. We justify that we all have sin in our lives, so who are we to judge? And that is a true statement. We all have sin in our lives, BUT the only difference between this sin and many other sins is the outright rebellion against God's Word. LGBTQ people do not admit that homosexuality is a sin against God's Seventh Commandment:

"Thou shalt not commit adultery."

If there's no admittance to the sin of homosexuality or any other sin, then according to the Bible, there is no forgiveness of sin (1 John 1:9).

We, as a church, must remember that even though we love everyone, God's Word never changes. His law remains the same. We, as a church, cannot accept that which God rejects, no matter how emotionally caught up we are with individuals we love. Sin cannot be affirmed by the Christian church with God's blessings. The Scripture is plain: God's Word never changes. Malachi 3:6 says,

"FOR I AM THE LORD, I CHANGE NOT" (emphasis added).

Sins such as adultery and homosexuality cannot change with

time or culture. They represent the breaking of the Seventh Commandment of

"Thou shalt not commit adultery."

Try as we might, God's Ten Commandment law can never be changed by man. Each generation seems to be getting farther and farther away from God and His Word. And what's worse is many Christian churches are supporting this deception!

2 Timothy 4:3-4 addresses this problem:

"For the time will come when they will not endure sound doctrine; but after their own lusts shall they heap to themselves teachers, having itching ears; And they shall turn away their ears from the truth, and shall be turned unto fables."

This is a Scripture that now represents "present truth." It is happening now in many Christian churches!

I'm amazed that the Bible has stood the test of time for thousands of years, and to my knowledge, there have been no Christian groups, pastors, or theologians refuting texts such as Romans chapter 1, Leviticus 18:22, 1 Corinthians. 6:9-11, etc. Previously, no pastor would dare stand up before his congregation and reinterpret Scriptures about open sin against God! They are now boldly substituting error for the truth because many in their congregations have rejected sound Bible doctrine in search of teachers appealing to their own lust of the flesh.

I recently heard a theologian reinterpreting the book of Romans telling his flock that perhaps Paul's teaching against open sin (including homosexuality) only applied to the culture of his day. Therefore, Romans chapter 1 would not be applicable today regarding homosexuality and transgender lifestyles. This either means that the Bible has been misinterpreted for thousands of years or someone has recently discovered "new light." I assure you the problem lies with the ministers who are not willing to stand up for the truth of God's Word.

1Timothy 4:1-2 states:

> "Now the Spirit speaketh expressly, that in the latter times some shall depart from the faith, giving heed to seducing spirits, and doctrines of devils; Speaking lies in hypocrisy; having their conscience seared with a hot iron..."

This is now present truth. It is no longer a prophecy for the end times. We are living in the end times.

When the Christian church affirms that which God rejects, we will pay the consequences of playing God! Man CANNOT place himself on the throne of God and accept rebellion against God's own Ten Commandment law in the Christian church. When that happens, the Holy Spirit leaves, and those churches guilty of affirming what God describes as an abomination now become followers of Satan! That's why, at the beginning of this book, I wrote that to know and understand the definition of sin and its consequences is a matter of eternal life or death.

As Christians, we should counteract the counterfeit instead of being silent on these issues. Openly "gay" church members are growing by leaps and bounds in many Christian churches. Many church leaders have not been willing to stand against the affirmation of open sin in the church. Why? Because the vast majority of church members are NOT standing up against this reshaping of biblical values.

LGBTQ PUSHES ITS AGENDA THE HARDEST

Have you noticed that other open sins, such as heterosexual couples living together outside of marriage, are not getting the same aggressive push for affirmation by many Christians as the LGBTQ group? I have. Let me address adultery, for example. Adultery is also a sin. Any sexual relationship outside of the biblical model of a man and a woman (husband and wife) is adultery.

To be clear, I'm not making any excuses or dancing around the fact that adultery is a sexual sin. Like homosexuality, adultery is also a sin of lust and is not of God. Please follow me: homosexuality and adultery are sins that can be forgiven when confessed to God. But again, the key point is sins that are confessed to God.

In my 40 years of ministry, I've yet to meet with an admitted adulterer who denies that adultery is a sin. The same applies to an alcoholic, a drug addict, a thief, a murderer, a rapist, etc. They all acknowledge that their vices come under the biblical heading of "sin" against God's law. Most Christians accept the Bible's definition of adultery as a sin when either the male or female commits sexual acts with someone outside the marriage bed God ordained.

Open adultery is not tolerated by most Christian churches that I know of. There is no adultery group protesting the Christian church for calling out the sin of adultery. People understand the biblical position of the church and either comply with the Seventh Commandment or leave the church. They do not demand that the church affirm adultery as a typical Christian lifestyle. And as of yet, I haven't seen anyone trying to promote the sin of adultery into being affirmed by the church. Have you?

The Bible and its position on adultery and homosexuality are very clear. Thankfully, we don't have to be neurosurgeons or Bible scholars to understand it. We just have to be seekers of truth.

Though all sin is destructive, I do believe that some sins are more harmful to the body of Christ than others. The LGBTQ community has declared war on Christianity by their mission to indoctrinate our young children with lies about the sin of homosexuality. The LGBTQ community is the only group I'm aware of that has successfully bombarded our public schools with hundreds of "queer" books encouraging students to experiment in homosexual encounters with other students of the same sex as early as grade school! And in many states, the government is supporting underage children to be able to have sex reassignment operations without the parents' consent! Think about it: the current laws of the land don't even allow underage young people to buy cigarettes, alcohol, or even get a tattoo or driver's license. But many of these states make it lawful to get sex reassignment surgery even without parents' consent under the heading of gender-affirming health care!

If the LGBTQ movement succeeds in this spiritual battle of the indoctrination of our children, the church of God will be adversely affected for generations to come! It's past time for the Christian church to stand up against the affirmation of open sin, such as the LGBTQ group.

Now, let me be clear. If they lived their lives separately without demanding affirmation from the Christian church, I would not be writing this book. They know that if they can influence a significant number of young people to accept/affirm them now, the next generation of Christians will consider LGBTQ as a totally normal group of members and leaders in the church.

Remember, the devil needs our cooperation in order to deceive us. Deception is a choice to accept his lies over and above the truth of God's Word. We will not stand before God on Judgment Day and blame the devil for deceiving us. We will not be deceived as long as we desire truth and keep our eyes on Jesus and Him crucified. John 7:17 says,

> "If any man will do his will, he shall know of the doctrine, whether it be of God, or whether I speak of myself."

And Luke 9:23 states,

> "And he said to them all, If any man will come after me, let him deny himself, and take up his cross daily, and follow me. For whosoever will save his life shall lose it: but whosoever will lose his life for my sake, the same shall save it."

The concept of "dying to self" is found throughout the New Testament. It simply means that, as human beings, we understand that there is no hope of eternal life without Christ. Our salvation is 100% found in Jesus Christ and Him crucified. Salvation is conditional. Thus, we take up our cross and follow Christ. Dying to self is part of being born again; the old self dies, and the new self comes to life (John 3:3-7). This is part of the process of sanctification.

For the Christian, coming to Christ is essential in obtaining eternal life, but sanctification is the work of a lifetime. As humans, we will fail God from time to time, but through daily study of His Word and prayer, we become more like Jesus than we were when we started our Christian journey. This is why it is so important to realize that we are all born with a sinful fallen nature and can only be saved by the blood of Jesus. Acts 4:12 says,

> "Neither is there salvation in any other: for there is none other name under heaven given among men, whereby we must be saved."

IN CONCLUSION.........

Do we deny church membership and leadership positions to those who live in open sin and rebellion to God's Ten Commandment law? The answer is "yes." We cannot affirm their sins by including them in church membership and leadership. Suppose the Christian church affirms the open sin of the LGBTQ community or an unmarried heterosexual couple living together, for instance. In that case, the church will have to affirm all open sin, which means there will be no more sin-- period! The church cannot choose one sin over another to attempt to affirm/forgive. So that means the church would be obligated to attempt to forgive and affirm all unrepented open sinners such as child molesters, murderers, rapists, drug abusers, and so on.

As we already said, man cannot change God's law. The Christian church has NO authority from God to affirm any open sin. This includes the unconfessed sins of the LGBTQ community in breaking God's Seventh Commandment of "Thou shalt not commit adultery!"

In the world's eyes, the LGBTQ community has accomplished pushing its agenda with great success. They can openly have "pride" marches. They can build a coalition of supporters, connect themselves with the civil rights movement, and even influence our public schools to promote their ungodly agenda to innocent children as young as the 2nd and 3rd graders. But, all of this does not impress or move God one iota to change His Ten Commandment law! He cannot and will not change it for you, me, or the LGBTQ movement! Even with the Supreme Court's victory in making same-sex marriage the law of the land in 2015, they cannot, and I emphasize CANNOT, change one jot or tittle of God's law! God will not allow sin or rebellious sinners to enter into the kingdom of heaven.

Please listen closely: we are not talking here about a group that stumbles, falls occasionally, and comes back to the foot of the cross. No! This group denies they are living in sin, so there is no need to ask Jesus to forgive them of their sin. And, as I've already said, they have every right to believe what they want to about sin. But, as a church, we cannot allow their deception to chip away at the law of God that we Christians have committed to uphold.

It doesn't make any difference how much earthly support they have. They do not have God's support! No one will be in heaven without repentance and forgiveness. It's that simple! It's biblical. This is not a judgment call by me personally or anyone else. This is a "thus saith the Lord." Repentance and forgiveness were incorporated into the Plan of Salvation from the foundation of the world. All the hoop-la in the world by the LGBTQ movement will not escape the biblical fact that everyone, without exception, must humble themselves and turn from their wicked ways in order to be forgiven by our Creator God (2 Chronicles 7:14).

A TWO-FOLD APPEAL

Today, my appeal is two-fold. It is to those living in open sin against God and His law and those in the church to stand up and be counted as watchmen on the wall to ensure that God's church does not compromise with the world.

FIRST, TO THOSE CAUGHT UP IN SIN'S WEB: Living in open sin can indeed bring you temporary pleasure and satisfaction, but it leads to spiritual emptiness and separation from God. Sin entangles us, enslaves us, and robs us of the abundant life that Jesus offers. It is a heavy burden that weighs us down and prevents us from experiencing true freedom and joy, but there is hope in Jesus. In His love and mercy, He offers us forgiveness and redemption. He willingly gave His life on the cross to pay the price for our sins. Through His sacrifice, He provides us with a way to be reconciled with God and to have our sins washed away in the sea of forgetfulness! Everything you've ever done can be covered by His blood. If you turn to Jesus, this is what He says in John 6:37:

> "All that the Father giveth me shall come to me; and him that cometh to me, I will in no wise cast out."

Choose Jesus and discover the true joy and peace that can only be found in Him.

AND TO THE CHURCH: Today, I come before you with a fervent call to action—a call for the Christian church to rise up as watchmen on the wall, defending the timeless principles of the Bible. As watchmen, it is our responsibility to guard the truth, protect the integrity of our faith, and ensure that open sin does not find affirmation within our beloved church.

In a world where moral boundaries are often blurred, and cultural norms shift, it is imperative that we stand firm on the unchanging foundation of God's Word. Let us be unwavering in our commitment to upholding the teachings and principles that have guided us throughout history.

As watchmen, we must remain vigilant, discerning the influences that seek to infiltrate our churches. We must not succumb to the world's pressures but boldly proclaim the truth with love and compassion. Let us create an environment where sin is acknowledged but never endorsed or celebrated.

Brothers and sisters, our role as watchmen requires both courage and conviction. We must be willing to speak up when the principles of the Bible are compromised, even when it is uncomfortable or unpopular. We must strive to foster a community where accountability and grace coexist—a place where sinners find refuge, forgiveness, and transformation.

It is not our duty to judge or condemn but to guide, support, and gently lead one another towards righteousness. Let us embody Christ's love, extending a helping hand to those who are struggling while also upholding the truth that sets us free.

Together, as united members of the body of Christ, let us commit ourselves to prayer, seeking divine wisdom and discernment while remaining anchored in the unchanging truth of God's Word.

May our churches be beacons of light in a world that is desperately searching for hope and meaning. Let us be known for our unwavering dedication to the principles of the Bible, not allowing open sin to be affirmed within our midst. By doing so, we can inspire others to seek the transformative power of God's love and experience the abundant life He has promised.